001. Louis-Jacques-Mandé Daguerre. *Boulevard du Temple, Paris,* c. 1838.

002. Robert Cornelius (attrib.). *Seated Couple,* c. 1840.

003. Hippolyte Bayard.
Self Portrait as a Drowned Man, 1840.

004. William Henry Fox Talbot.
"The Haystack" from *The Pencil of Nature,* 1844.

005. Jean-Baptiste Sabatier-Biot.
Louis-Jacques-Mandé Daguerre, 1844.

006. Photographer Unknown.
Daguerrotype of a Gentleman, c. 1845.

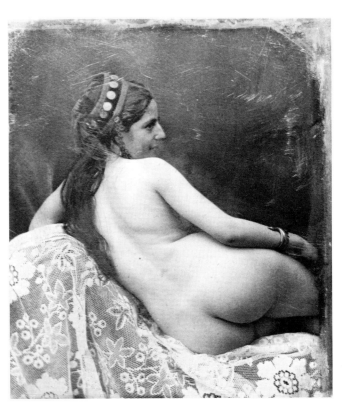

007. Gustav Oehme. *Three Young Girls,* c. 1845.

008. Photographer Unknown. *Académie,* c. 1845.

009. David Octavius Hill and Robert Adamson.
The Misses Binny and Monro, c. 1845.

010. John Plumbe. *Capitol Building,
Washington, D.C.,* 1845–46.

011. Thomas Easterly. *Keokuk, Sauk Chief,* 1847.

012. Photographer Unknown. *Frederick Douglass,* 1847.

4

014. Photographer Unknown.
Goldminers, California, c. 1850.

013. Photographer Unknown.
Edgar Allan Poe, 1849.

015. Photographer Unknown. *Portrait of an Unidentified
African-American Woman,* c. 1850.

5

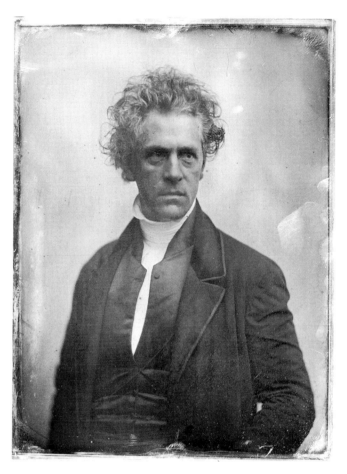

016. Albert Sands Southworth and
Josiah Johnson Hawes. *Rollin Heber Neal,* c. 1850.

017. Maxime du Camp.
The Colossus of Abu-Simbel, Nubia, 1850.

018. Frederick Coombs.
Montgomery Street, San Francisco, 1850.

019. Antoine François Claudet.
The Geography Lesson, c. 1850.

020. Antoine François Claudet.
Family Group, c. 1852.

021. Platt D. Babbitt. *The Niagara Falls,* c. 1853

022. Thomas Keith. *Bakerhouse Close,*
Canongate, Edinburgh, c. 1854.

023. Roger Fenton. *A Quiet Day in the Mortar Battery,*
1855.

024. Genevieve-Elisabeth Disdérí.
Interior of St. Mathieu, c. 1856.

025. Francis Frith. *Interior Hall of Columns,*
Karnac, c. 1857.

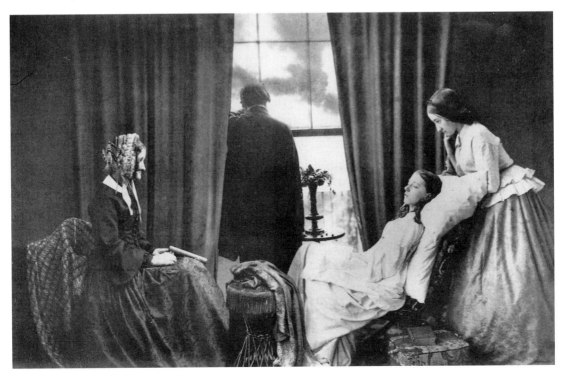

026. H. P. Robinson. *"Fading Away,"* 1858.

027. William M. Grundy. "The Country Stile," 1859.

028. Lewis Carroll.
Alice Liddell as "The Beggar Maid," c. 1859.

029. Oscar Gustav Rejlander. *Lewis Carroll
(Rev. Charles L. Dodgson)*, 1863.

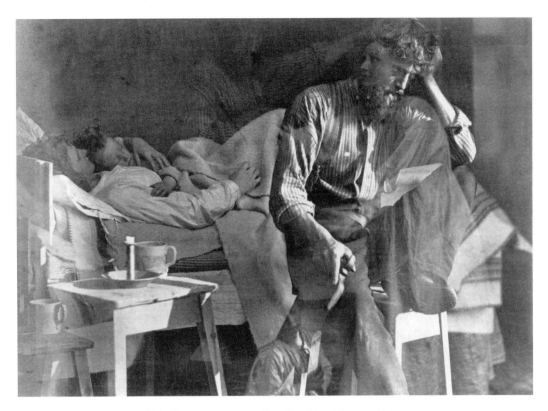

030. Oscar Gustav Rejlander. *Hard Times,* 1860.

031. James Wallace Black. *Boston from the Air,* 1860.

032. Mathew Brady. *The Lincoln "Cooper Union" Portrait,* February 27, 1860.

033. Mathew Brady. *Robert E. Lee [General Custis Lee, left, and Colonel Walter Taylor, right]*, 1865.

034. Mathew Brady. *Clara Barton, c. 1866.*

035. T. [Timothy] H. O'Sullivan. *"The Harvest of Death"— battlefield of Gettysburg,* July 1863.

036. T. [Timothy] H. O'Sullivan. *Richmond, Virginia,* 1865.

037. Photographer Unknown. *Dead Confederate Soldier in Trench Beyond Cheveaux-de-frise, Petersburg, Virginia,* 1865.

038. Photographer Unknown. *John Wilkes Booth,* n.d.

039. George M. Barnard.
Ruins of Charleston, S.C., c. 1865.

040. Photographer Unknown. *Powder Monkey, "U.S.S. New Hampshire," off Charleston, S.C.,* c. 1865.

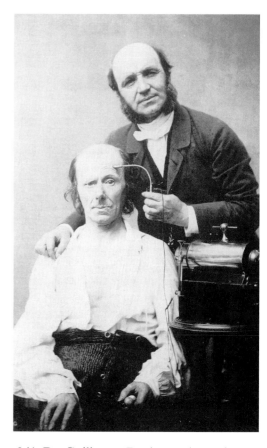

041. Dr. Guillaume Duchenne de Boulogne.
Faradisation du muscle frontal, 1862

042. Julia Margaret Cameron. *Ellen Terry,* 1864.

043. Julia Margaret Cameron. *Paul and Virginia,* 1864.

044. Lady Clementina Hawarden.
Photographic Study, c. 1863.

045. Lewis M. Rutherford. *Moon,* March 4, 1865.

046. Alexander Gardner. *Lewis Payne, One of the Lincoln Conspirators before His Execution,* 1865.

047. Alexander Gardner. *[Execution of the Lincoln Assassination Conspirators], The Scaffold,* 1865.

048. Philippos Margaritis. *Untitled [Acropolis]*, 1865.

049. Carleton Watkins. *El Capitan*, c. 1866.

050. Napoleon Sarony. *Adah Isaacs Menkin as Mazeppa,* 1866.

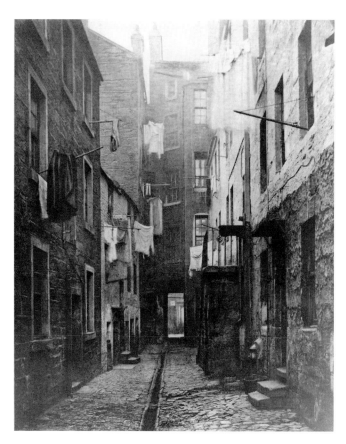

051. Thomas Annan. *"Close No. 75 High Street," Old Closes and Streets of Glasgow,* 1868.

052. John L. Dunmore and George Critcherson. *Sailing Ships in an Ice Field,* 1869.

053. Andrew J. Russell. *Meeting of the Rails, Promontory Point, Utah,* 1869.

054. Félix Bonfils. *Jerusalem, Damascus Gate,* c. 1870.

055. William Henry Jackson. *Yellowstone Canyon*, 1871.

056. Mélandri. *Sarah Bernhardt with her self-portrait bust*, c. 1876.

057. Tourtin. *Sarah Bernhardt, from Galerie Contemporarie*, 1877.

058. John Thomson. *Junkshop in London,* 1876.

059. John Thomson. *"The Crawlers,"*
Street Life in London, 1877.

060. Carlo Naya. *Venizia; Palaces Foscari, Giustinian and*
Rezzonico, on the Grand Canal, 1875.

061. Etienne Carjat. *Charles Baudelaire* from *Galerie Contemporarie,* 1878

062. Photographer Unknown. *Brooklyn Bridge under Construction,* c. 1878.

063. L. M. Melender and Brother. *The Haunted Lane,* c. 1880.

064. Photographer Unknown. *North African (?) in Costume,* c. 1880.

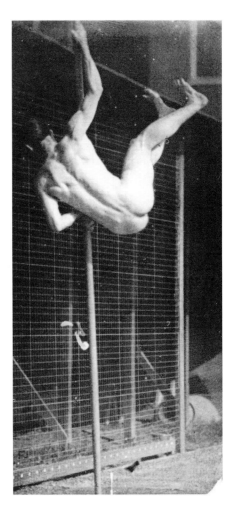

065. Heinrich Tönnies. *Four Young Blacksmiths,* c. 1881.

066. Eadweard Muybridge. *Pole Vaulter,* 1885.

067. George Bretz. *Breaker Boys, Eagle Hill Colliery,* c. 1884.

068. Thomas Eakins. *History of a Jump,* 1884–85.

069. Paul Nadar. *The Photographer's Wife,* 1853.

070. Paul Nadar. *Nadar Interviews the Centenarion M.-E. Chevreul,* 1886.

071. Peter Henry Emerson. *Gathering Water Lilies,* 1886

072. Peter Henry Emerson. *"East Coast Fisherman,"*
Norfolk Broads, c. 1886.

073. Jacob A. Riis. *Bandits' Roost, New York,* 1888.

074. Jacob A. Riis. *Sabbath Eve in a Coal Cellar,*
Ludlow Street, early 1890s.

075. Alfred Stieglitz. *The Terminal (New York)*, 1893.

076. Frederick Fargo Church. *George Eastman on Board the S.S. Gallia,* February 1890.

077. Alfred Stieglitz. *The Steerage,* 1907.

078. Charles Dudley Arnold. *Basin and the Court of Honor,* 1893.

079. Paul Martin. *The Magazine Seller, Ludgate Circus, London,* c. 1895.

080. Arnold Genthe. *The Fish Dealer's Daughter,* c. 1895.

081. Edward S. Curtis. *Princess Angeline,* 1896.

082. Edward S. Curtis. *Washo Baskets,* c. 1924.

083. Robert Demachy. *"Primavera,"* c. 1896.

084. Frances Benjamin Johnson. *Self-Portrait (as New Woman),* c. 1896.

085. Frederick H. Hollyer. *Aubrey Beardsley,* 1896.

086. Frances Benjamin Johnson.
Hampton Institute science class, 1899.

087. Emile Zola. *Denise Sitting, Doll in her Arms,*
c. 1897–1902.

088. Adam Clark Vroman. *Nawquistewa,*
Hopi Indian, Oraibi, 1901.

089. Adam Clark Vroman. *Mission, Santa Clara Pueblo,*
New Mexico, 1899.

090. Fred Boissonnas. *"Coming Home from the Theatre,"*
1900.

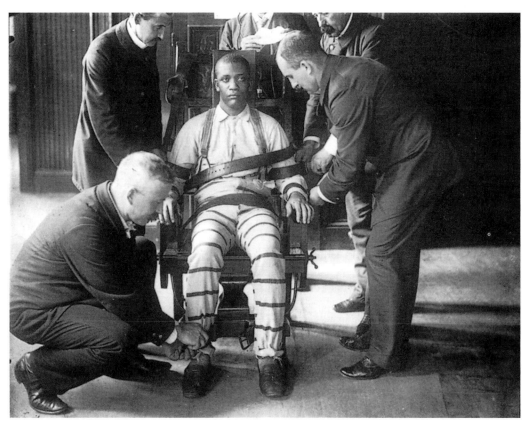

091. William M. Van der Weyde.
Electric Chair at Sing Sing, c. 1900

092. Charles B. Waite. *Doing the Washing in Mexico,* c. 1900.

093. Photographer Unknown.
Wedding Picture, 1901.

094. Photographer Unknown.
Wall Street, New York, c. 1900.

095. Gertrude Käsebier. *Portrait— Miss N. (Evelyn Nesbitt)*, 1902.

096. Edward Steichen. *Rodin*, 1902.

097. Edward Steichen. *The Flatiron*, 1905.

098. Edward Steichen. *Alfred Stieglitz at 291 [Fifth Avenue]*, 1915.

099. Frederick H. Evans. *The Sea of Steps—Wells Cathedral,* 1903.

100. Clarence H. White and Alfred Stieglitz. *Miss Thompson,* 1907.

101. Alfred Stieglitz. *The Steerage,* 1907.

102. Clarence H. White. *Nude,* c. 1909.

103. Alfred Stieglitz. *Portrait of Georgia O'Keeffe,* 1922.

104. Lewis W. Hine. *Carolina Cotton Mill,* 1908.

105. Herbert Ponting. *An Iceberg in Midsummer,*
Antarctica, 1910–1913.

106. Jacques Henri Lartigue.
Avenue du Bois de Boulogne, 1911.

107. Augustus Sherman. *Women from Guadeloupe, French West Indies, at Ellis Island,* 1911.

108. Alvin Langdon Coburn. *Miss Anderson,* 1908.

109. Alvin Langdon Coburn. *The House of a Thousand Windows, New York,* 1912.

110. Alvin Langdon Coburn. *Vortograph of Ezra Pound,* 1917.

111. E. J. Bellocq. "New Orleans Prostitute," from *Storyville Portraits,* c. 1913.

112. Alice Boughton. "Nude," from *Camera Work,* April 1909.

113. Elias Goldensky. *Male Nude,* c. 1915.

114. Paul Strand. *Blind Woman in New York,* 1915.

115. Paul Strand. *Abstractions, Porch Shadows, Connecticut*, 1915.

116. Baron Adolph de Meyer. *A Wedding Dress, Modeled by Helen Lee Worthing*, 1920.

117. Photographer Unknown.
Wright Brothers Postcard, 1915.

118. Charles Sheeler. *Bucks County Barn,* c. 1916.

119. Albert Renger-Patzsch. *Echeoeria,* 1922.

120. Man Ray. *Rayograph,* 1922.

121. Edward Weston. *Armco Steel, Ohio,* 1922.

122. Nickolas Muray. *Gloria Swanson,* c. 1922.

123. Imogen Cunningham. *Magnolia Blossom,* 1925.

124. Eugène Atget. *Avenue des Gobelins,* 1925.

125. Eugène Atget. *Prostitute, Paris,* 1920s.

126. Hugo Erfurth. *Käthe Kollwitz,* c. 1925.

127. James Van der Zee.
Future Expectations, c. 1925.

128. Karl Blossfeldt. *Chrysanthemum Parthenium
[Feverfew],* 1928.

129. Doris Ulmann. *South Carolina,* c. 1929–1930.

130. Dorothea Lange. *Migrant Mother, Nipomo, California,* 1936.

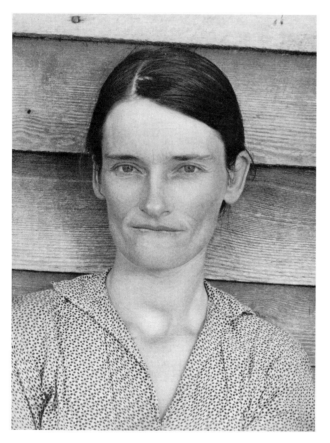

131. Walker Evans. *Allie Mae Burroughs, wife of Floyd Burroughs,* 1936.

132. Walker Evans. *Floyd Burroughs, cotton sharecropper, Alabama,* 1936.

133. Ben Shahn. *Cotton Pickers, Pulaski County, Arkansas,* 1935.

134. Walker Evans. *Sharecropper Bud Fields and family at home, Alabama,* 1936

135. Russell Lee. *Hidalgo County, Texas,* 1939.

136. Russell Lee. *Second Hand Tires, San Marcos, Texas,*
1940.

137. Dorothea Lange. *Dust Bowl Victims,* 1935–1941.

138. Gordon Parks. *Ella Watson (American Gothic),* 1942.

139. Marion Post Wolcott. *Family of Migrant Packinghouse Workers, Homestead, Florida,* 1939.

Index of Photographers (where identified)

Index of Sitters